5 SECONDS OF SUMMER

OFFICIAL POSTER COLLECTION

All rights reserved. No part of this product may be reproduced, stored in a retrieval system or transmitted, in any form or by any means, electric, digital, mechanical, photocopy, recording, or otherwise, without prior permission in writing from the publisher.

ISBN: 978-1-4650-4721-2

 ©2014 under license to Global Merchandising Services Ltd.

 BrownTrout Publishers, Inc.
The Calendar Company

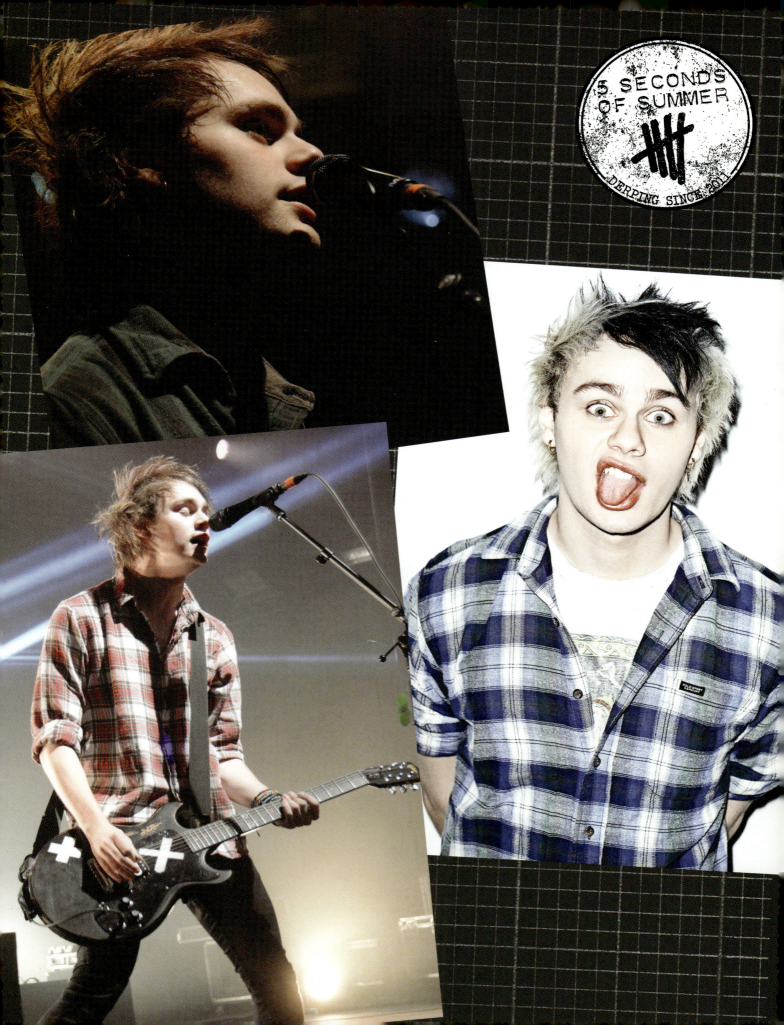